Published l

MW01170972

Copyright © 2021Aι

ISBN: 9761736631232

Cover design by Bonita Bly

Editorial service by Gifted Hands by Bonita

First Edition 2021

Printed in the United States of America

Dedicated To

My Mother Odessa L. Watson

And

My little Sister Annette Gibbs

Mother

Who always watches over me,
who knows the pit falls in the rugged road I tread?

A playmate who will always treat me kindly
who will field me what true happiness demands?

She will never let my feet stray into brambles blindly
Mother's just a bigger little girl who understands me.

She travelled in the path that's mine today.

A Mothers Love

A Mother love right from the start.
She holds me close to her heart.
The bond that grows will never falter.
Her love is so strong it will never alter.

She never feels that she has given enough.
For you she will always do her best.
Constantly working, there's no time to rest.

A hug and a kiss to help me along.
Always there when I need her nearby.
Gently wipes my eyes when I shed a tear.

Be gentle, be good, be helpful, be kind.

I Love You Mom

I will love you forever Mom.

The most wonderful mother,
You mean everything to me.

I thought of buying you flowers

But I knew you would prefer
A forever bouquet!

My Handprint

Here is my handprint,
Five fingers in all,
Outside they are short,
But the middle is tall,

You will find them on windows,
You can find them on the wall,
You will find the in the dirt
That will make a big mess,
For something so small.

So here is one now,
That you can't wipe away.

The Best Mom

You are the best Mom, from your head to your toes.
You are warm and soft as you hold me in your arms.
Smelling sweet like a rose.

When you leave the room your perfume
scent always remains in the room.

You are the best Mom always go out your way
to make sure I have everything that I need.

You made sure I had the best education,
provided meals for me three times a day,
and sometimes more if I wanted a snack.

The love I have for you Mom will always remain
In my heart.

You are the best Mom in the World no one
could every replace you.

My Angel

There are Angels God puts on this Earth.

Who care for us and guide us?
you can feel their love and gentleness
as they walk through life beside us.

They do great things for us every day
they whisper in our ears,
they even hold us in their hearts
when we are filled with all our fears.

They are always there to give a hug
and try to make us smile.
The treat us with respect and love,
they treat us like their child.

God blessed me with an Angel,
I'm proud to call my own.
She's been with me as I've grown.

You guided me the best you can,
you taught me like no other,
and I'm thankful I'm the Bless call you Mom.

To My Mom

What can I say about my mother?
An extraordinary mom like no other,
Whenever I need you, you're always there.
You listen, understand, and show that you care.

But Mom, there's just so much more to you.
It's hard to describe the feelings I feel.
My love for you, Mom, is deep and real.

I appreciate you more than I ever could say.

Wonderful Mother

When God made you, he made a
Wonderful Mother.

He made your smile of the sunshine,

He molded your heart of pure gold.
And your eyes He placed bright shining stars'

In your cheek's fair roses, you see.
God made a wonderful mother,

And he gave that dear mother to me.

Mom You Are Special Gift from Above

For all you do
You do with love
You are so special a gift from God.

And, with all my heart
I want to say
I love you Mom

Mothers

Mothers gives her children steppingstones.
Her love is unconditional her heart has no bars.

Mothers teaches her children to be confident
and bold,
A special love to her children is more
valuable than silver or gold.

Mothers picks up her children
and wipes away their tears,
Mothers chases away monsters in the night
and silences their fears.

Mothers celebrates her children's
accomplishments in life,
She cries with them
when life becomes hard.

Mothers shares her love freely
with her tender love.

Mothers is one of God's greatest
gifts to you and me,
Her love will remain locked in
our heart and soul for all eternity.

You Are My Rose

Roses are red
Violets are blue
Sugar is sweet
And so are you!

The Best Mom

You have given me life
and showed me the light.
You gave me the strength to fight,
And difference of wrong from right.

When there are problems,
you always stayed and never walked away
You always picked me up along the way.

I'll always be proud to say,
you are the best.

I Love You Mom

A Mothers love is always pure
No trace of insecurity but a better cure.

A mother's love maybe strict

A mother's love is always true
It's all you need to get you through those
tough days

A mother's love can seem like hate

A mother's love is a shelter
in times of troubles, you don't have to fear

A mother's love is always there
in simple ways she'll show how much she cares

A mother's love can never compare
with anyone else's anywhere
it's is always here to stay

You Mean the World to Me

Your eyes, calm as leaves in the frost,
your eyes, sparked when I am disrespectful,

Your Heart, with mine always,
forgiving me,

Your Voice, soothing my fears,
praising me, calming me,
and helping me.

My Mothers Garden

She planted all the good things that
gave my life its start.
She turned me to the sunshine
and encouraged me
to dream, fostering and
nurturing the seeds of self-esteem.

When the winds and rains came,
she protected me enough,
but not too much because she knew
I needed to grow strong and tough.

I am my mother's garden.
I am her legacy and
I hope today she feels the love
reflected back from me.

You cuddle me

You cuddle me, kisses me, hug me,
and misses me pampers me,
praises me, always amazes me.

Washes my clothes for me,
tickles my toes for me,
giggles and talks with me,
and also goes on walks with me,

Sings sweet songs to me,
I am glad she belongs to me.

I am so glad you are my mother
that continues to cuddle me.

I've Learned So Much from You

When I was young, you helped me grow,
And taught me all I had to know.

About love, trust, faith and hope,

You may have thought I didn't hear,
Or maybe that you weren't quite clear.

But all the things you taught to me
were heed very carefully,

And now I want to thank you for
Your love, your care, and so much more!

Fingerprints

Fingerprints, Fingerprints, Fingerprints, everywhere!

On the windows and walls, even the chair!

You wipe them and scrub them and wash them away.

But on this day, they are here to stay.

With Courage and Faith

With courage and faith, you soar higher.
With endurance you fought with stress.
A never-ending effort to give your best.

You cross over valleys of defeat
Dream big for your children
Never thought to surrender
But to push yourself further.

It is my pleasure to let you know
That I've been blessed with a mom like you
For all the things you've done.
I'm proud to call you mom!

My Teacher

My mother is my first teacher
She taught me everything I know
She says that alphabets start with A-B-C
And numbers start with 1-2-3.

She said that Earth revolves in the sun.
But my whole world revolves on her.
With everything she has done
From birth till now, my life belongs to her.

On your day, my love continues.
My love for you will never lose.

The Best Mom

My mom is the best Mom
She's sweet as she can be.
When I need some help, I know
She's always there for me.

My mom loves me all the time,
Even when I'm a pest.
She always takes good care of me.
My Mother is the best.

Thinking About You Mom

You're my past, future, my all, my everything
my lovely mom who is there when I open my eyes.

My laughs, my frowns, my ups, my downs
It's a feeling that I get from my mom
when I think of love,
I think about you.

I Love My Mom

I love my mom for all that she does.
I'll hug and kiss my mom because she loves me too!
My mom feed me, and
teach me to play.
Smile because I love you.

Dependable Mom

You're a dependable source of comfort.
You're my fusion when I fall.

You help in times of trouble.
You support me whenever I call.

I love you more than you know.
You have my total respect.

If I have my choice of mothers.
You'd be the one I'd select.

Diamonds

If I could give you diamonds
for each tear you cried for me.
There will be so many that you would
not have enough room to put
them in your jewelry box.

If I could give you rubies for the heartache
that you've known

If I could give you pearls
for the wisdom that you've shown.

Then you'll have a treasure, mother,
that would mount up to the skies

That would almost match the sparkle
in your kind and loving eyes.

But I have no pearls, no diamonds,
As I'm sure you're well aware

So, I'll give you gifts more precious
My devotion, love and care.

Mother

Mother you taught me to pray,
To love and serve God every day,

You ran to help me when I fell,
And would say some pretty story tell,
Then kiss the place to make it well.

How could I ever cease to be?
Affectionate and kind to thee
Who was so kind to me?
My Mother!

You Understands Me

My mother always understands the things I say and do.
She overlooks each of my faults,
She finds the best in me.

My Mother's love is a special love,
it inspires me each day.
She spreads her joy and happiness,
in her warm and caring way.

My Mother's all these things and more,
there's no greater treasure known.
The most precious Mother in all the world.

Special Joys

Of all the special joys in life.
The big ones and the small,

My mother's love and tenderness are the
Greatest of them all.

I'm Blessed

I asked my friends what makes their mom great.
They told me that she was their mate.

They asked me why my mom's the best,
I gave them this list and told them.

Cooking dinner, cuddles, play,
Singing, dancing music all day.

Driving, walking riding a bike,
My mom knows exactly what I like.

Homework, reading, computer fun
Endless weekends watching me run.

Solving puzzles, block towers that sway,
Keeping up with me all day!

Tucking me in with a book and a song,
Even though her day was long.

This is why Mom, I have to say,
I love you so much.
I'm Blessed.

Undying Love

My Mother is an undying love,
A love beyond compare,
The one you take your troubles to
She is the one who really cares.

My Mother is all of this and more.

I love my mother very much.

Only If Roses Grow in Heaven

If Roses grown in Heaven,
Lord, please pick a bunch for me,
Place them in my Mother's arms
and tell her they're from me.

Tell Her I love her and miss her,
And when she turns to smile,
Place a kiss upon her cheek
And hold her for a while.

Because remembering her is easy,
I do it every day,
but there's an ache within my heart
That will never go away.

My Mother's Love

Her love is like an island in life's ocean,
vest and wide

A peaceful, quiet shelter
From the wind, the rain, the tide.

This bounds on the north by Hope,
By Patience on the West,

Above it like a beacon light
Shine Faith, Truth and Prayer.
And through the changing scenes of life I
Find a haven there.

Mother's

They were lovely, all the mothers
of the days of long ago,
With their gentle, quiet faces
And their hair as white as snow.

They were middle-aged at forty,
At fifty donned lace caps
And at sixty clung to shoulder shawls
And loved that little naps.

But I love the modern mother
Who can share in all our joys,
And who understands the problems
Of her growing girls and boys.

She may boast she's older,
but her heart is twenty-three…
My glorious bright-eyed mother
Who is keeping young with me?

My Mother

Who fed me from her gentle breast?
And hushed me in her arms to rest,
And on my cheek sweet kisses?

When sleep forsook my open eye,
Who was it sung sweet lullaby?
And rocked me that I should not cry?

Who sat and watched my infant head?
When sleeping in my cradle bed,
And tears of sweet affection shed?

When pain and sickness made me cry,
Who gazed upon my heavy eye,
And wept, for fear that I should die?

Who ran to help me when I fell?
And would some pretty story tell,
Or kiss the part to make it well?

Who taught my infant lips to pray,
To love God's holy word and day,
And walk-in wisdom's pleasant way?

Continued……….

And can I ever cease to be
Affectionate and kind to thee
Who was so very kind to me?

Oh, no, the thought I cannot bear.
And if God please my life to spare
I hope I shall reward thy care,

When thou art feeble, old and gray,
My healthy arms shall be they stay,
And I will soothe they pains away,

And when I see thee hang thy head,
Twill be my turn to watch thy bed,
And tears of sweet affection shed

My Heart

For all that you have given me,
I can return but love.

All I can return but love for you.
Whose unmoved faith my heart did move.

And gave me hope and passion.
And loved me till I turned to love.

Whose moved faith did my heart move.
The mother of my heart.

Who loved me till I turned to love?
And I became the soul I would.

The mother of my heart.
And I became the soul I would
For all that you have given me.

My Mother is always with me

She's the whisper of the leaves as you walk
down the street.

She's the smell of certain foods you remember,
flowers you pick and perfume that she wore.

She's the cool had on your brow when you're
not feel well.

She's your breath in the air on a cold winter's day.

She is the sound of the rain that lulls you to
sleep, the colors of a rainbow.

My Mother lives inside my laughter,

A mother shows every emotion,
happiness, sadness, excitement, joy, sorrow

Continued………..

and all the while, hoping
and praying you will only know
the good feelings in life.

She's the place you came from,
your first home, and she's the map
you follow with ever step you take.

She's your first love; your first friend,
even your first enemy,
but nothing on earth can separate you.
Not time, not space, not death.

My Daughter Don't Mourn for Me

My daughter, please don't mourn for me,
I'm still here, though you don't see.
I'm right by your side each night and day.
And with your heart I long to stay.

My body is gone, but I'm always nearby,
I'm everything you feel, see or hear.
My spirit is free, but I'll never depart,
as long as you keep me alive in you hear.

I'll never wander out of your sight,
I'm the brightest star on a Summer night.
I'll never be beyond your reach,
I'm the warm, moist sand when you're at the beach.
I'm the colorful leaves when Fall comes around,
and the pure white snow that blankets the ground.

I'm the beautiful flowers of which you're so fond.
The clear, cool water in a quiet pond.
I'm the first bright blossom you'll see in the Spring,
the first warm rain drop that April will bring.

I'm the first ray of light when the sun starts to shine,
and you'll see that the face in the moon is mine.
When you start thinking there's no one to love you.
You can talk to me through the Lord above you.

Mom I Miss You

Mom, for every time I have let you down
For every time I made you frown

I know it is too late for an apology
But still, I want to say sorry

Like a fool I never realized the value
Or having a loving mother like you

I know you wanted me to be my best

I realize you wanted me to outline the rest

I promise to be the best person I can be

I promise to be the winner that you saw in me

It won't go in van, it won't escape your eyes

I know you will be watching on me from the skies

My Best Friend

Best friends forever mom and me
Picking flowers and climbing trees.

A shoulder to cry on secrets to share
Warm hearts and hands that really care.

Shopping at the mall every weekend
Our Dinner dates that meant a lot to me.

Going to the Casino you taught me
how to save money
And not gamble it away.

You will always be my best friend even though
You are not here anymore.

Well, your physical body is no longer her.
Your spirit will remain in my heart.

A Mother Just Like You

I just want to let you know
You mean the world to me
Only a heart as dear as yours
Would give so unselfishly

The many things you've done
All the times that you were there
Help me know deep down inside
How much you really care

Even though I might not say
I appreciate all you do
Richly blessed is how I feel
Having a mother just like you

Silent Tear

Just close your eyes and you will see
All the memories that you have of me

Just sit and relax and you will find
I'm really still there inside your mind

Don't cry for me know I'm gone
For I am in the land of song

There is no pain, there is no fear
So, dry away that silent tear

Don't think of me in the dark and cold

For here I am, no longer old
I'm in that place that's filled with
love
Known to you all, as "up above"

My wonderful Mother

God made a wonderful mother,
A mother who never grows old.

He made her smile of the sunshine,
And He molded her heart of pure gold.

In her eyes He placed bright shining stars,
In her cheeks, fair roses you see.

God made that wonderful mother,
And He gave that dear mother to me.

The Cord

We are connected, my child and I,
By an invisible cord not seen by the eye.

It's not liked the cord that connects us till birth
This cord can't be seen by any on Earth.

This cord does it's work right from the start,
It binds us together attached to my heart.

I know that it's there though no one can see
The invisible cord from my child to me.

The strength of this cord is hard to describe,
It can't be destroyed; it can't be denied.

It's stronger than any cord man could create,
It withstands the test, can hold any weight.

And though you are gone,
though you're not here with me,
The cord is still there, but no can see.

Continued............

It pulls at my heart, I am bruised I am sore,
But this cord is my lifeline as never before.

I am thankful that God connects us this way
A mother and child, death can't take it away!

My Precious Mother

Mom you've given me so much,
Love from your heart
And the warmth of your touch.
The gift of life and you're a friend to me.
We have a very special bond which only
Comes from
I'm sure you agree.

As a child I would say, Mom, I love you,
Now you're my Mother so dear
I love you even more with each and
Every new year.

If I could had chosen,
I would have picked no other.
Then for you to be my lifelong friend and
precious Mother.

Best Friends

Best friend's forever mom,
and me picking flowers, and
climbing trees.

A shoulder to cry on secrets to share
Warm hearts and hands that realty care.

Bonita Bly is a native of Boston, Massachusetts.
Through many trials and tribulations,
Bonita kept her faith and used prayer as a tool
to overcome many obstacles in life.

Over the years, God has provided Bonita with many
opportunities to share her testimony
and the life-changing message
of the Word of God.

She believes and teaches that regardless of a
person's background or past mistakes.

God has a place for them and can help
them on their path
To enjoying life path to enjoying life.

Bonita is fueled by a passion to
fulfill God's mandate
for these turbulent times.

Her thrust on character building by merging
spirituality with everyday living provokes people
to pursue a life of integrity.

Wherever she goes, Bonita exhorts and encourages
her listeners to deepen their intimacy with God
and arise to their divine calling and destiny.

Bonita is a two-time cancer survivor have never
had chemo nor radiation
she stood on the word of God.
Trusting God to heal her.

Bonita is married and a proud mother
of two handsome young men.

She is a graduate of Bethel Bible Institute,
Keys of the Kingdom School of the Prophets,
Ezra Institute of Apologetics.

Bonita was ordained as an Elder in 2007.

Bonita is the Author of:
Prayers That Never End/Pray Without Ceasing,
Woman of Strength book and
Woman of Strength Prayer Journal,
Enjoy Your Journey with the Lord,
Meditate on My Word, and
A Fathers Connection, and
Contributing Author of Destined to Win Book

Made in the USA
Columbia, SC
03 May 2023

15996428R00030